# BOREDOM BASHERS

MY AWESOME ACTIVITY BOOK

ARCTURUS

ARCTURUS

This edition published in 2011 by Arcturus Publishing Limited
26/27 Bickels Yard, 151–153 Bermondsey Street,
London SE1 3HA

ISBN: 978-1-84837-512-3
CH001410EN
Supplier 06, Date 0311, Print Run 896

Printed in Singapore

# Dinosaur Duo

There are two identical dinosaurs in this group.
Look carefully at all the images and draw a circle around the two that are exactly the same.

# Growing Wonder

Here's a mystery picture for you to identify.
Just draw what you see in each of the numbered boxes below into the
blank boxes that have the same number on the opposite page.

| 1 | 2 | 3 |
|---|---|---|
| | | |
| 4 | 5 | 6 |
| | | |
| 7 | 8 | 9 |
| | | |

# Fairytale Fuddle

Hidden in this word grid are the fairytale characters listed below. Look up, down, across and diagonally in both directions in the word grid and circle all that you find.

| D | T | I | P | N | B | H | L | I | H | Y | J | D | G | H |
|---|---|---|---|---|---|---|---|---|---|---|---|---|---|---|
| I | S | H | K | I | N | L | U | E | J | C | D | C | A | W |
| A | N | P | U | P | U | R | U | Q | Z | D | H | N | Z | Z |
| M | O | P | T | M | I | A | N | I | B | N | S | V | C | R |
| R | W | C | P | N | B | K | V | W | Q | E | U | O | F | N |
| E | W | N | K | M | F | E | R | Y | L | B | C | P | B | A |
| M | H | T | D | R | J | E | L | A | A | X | F | A | A | P |
| E | I | D | O | O | H | G | N | I | D | I | R | D | E | R |
| L | T | L | S | Z | S | D | T | C | N | E | E | F | H | E |
| T | E | Z | P | R | G | U | X | Z | O | A | N | W | A | T |
| T | W | N | L | R | O | O | W | M | T | J | N | R | Z | E |
| I | M | W | E | S | T | V | F | O | T | L | Q | W | B | P |
| L | Y | T | C | I | N | D | E | R | E | L | L | A | V | E |
| Z | E | D | R | A | E | B | E | U | L | B | F | E | Z | I |
| L | E | K | Z | I | F | J | I | B | G | Y | V | E | F | C |

CINDERELLA
PETER PAN
SNOW WHITE

BLUE BEARD
LITTLE MERMAID
RED RIDING HOOD

HANSEL AND GRETEL
RAPUNZEL
THUMBELINA

# Memory Test

Study this picture carefully for one minute,
then turn the page to answer some questions.

# Questions

How many things can you remember about the
picture on the previous page? No peeking!

**1.** What is the time showing on the table clock?

**2.** How many pencils are there?

**3.** Is there a dictionary among the books?

**4.** Is the computer on or off?

**5.** What is sitting on top of the computer?

**6.** What is hanging over the back of the chair?

**7.** Is there a book shelf?

**8.** Are there flowers in the vase?

**9.** Is it winter or spring?

**10.** Is there a snail on the window sill?

# Seven Steps

Starting from the top, move down each step adding one letter from the bottom row as you go, then rearrange all the letters around the 'A' to make a new word each time.

|   |   |   |   | A |   |   |   |
|---|---|---|---|---|---|---|---|
|   |   |   | A |   |   |   |   |
|   |   | A |   |   |   |   |   |
|   |   |   |   |   | A |   |   |
|   |   |   |   | A |   |   |   |
|   |   |   |   |   |   | A |   |
| M | A | S | T | E | R | S |   |

# Guess Who?

Here's a mystery picture for you to identify.
Just draw what you see in each of the numbered boxes below into the
blank boxes that have the same number on the opposite page.

| | | |
|---|---|---|
| **1** | **2** | **3** |
| **4** | **5** | **6** |
| **7** | **8** | **9** |

# Letter Leads

These letters spell a word when they are put in the right order. Track each letter along its path, then write it in its correct place to find out what the word is.

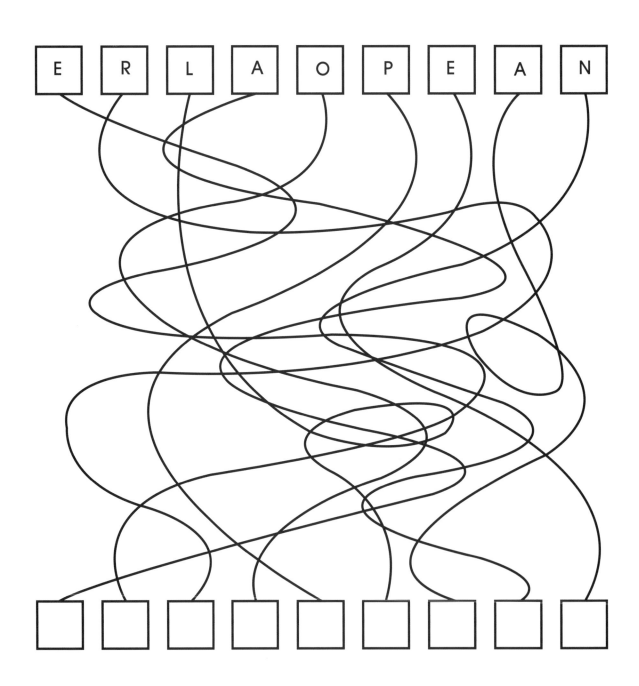

# Parallel or Not?

Are your eyes playing tricks? Look sharp and decide
if these lines are parallel or not!

# Mum and Me

What fun it is to go food shopping with mum!
Can you help us find all the items on our list that are hidden in this picture?

Ace of spades

Book

Carpet

Conch shell

Graph

Skateboard

Sweater

Tennis racket

Wallet

Watermelon slice

# Criss-Cross

How good are you at reading pictures? You had better be good!
Use the visual clues to fill in the words correctly in this picture crossword.

1. c h a r i

**Across**

① (chair)

④ (eggs)

③ (king)

⑦ (mittens)

**Down**

① (boat)

② (rollerblade)

⑤ (skunk)

⑥ (star)

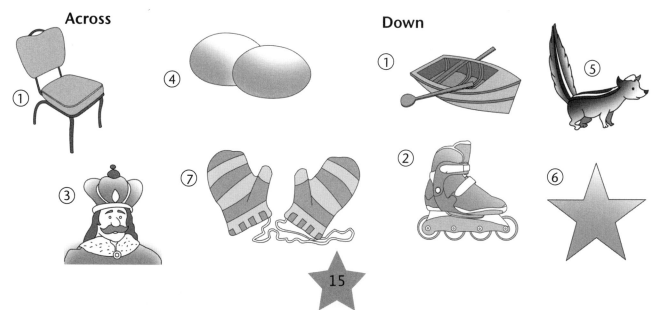

15

# Double Scoops

There are two identical ice-creams in this group.
Look carefully at the pictures and draw a circle around the two that are exactly the same.

# Middle Muddle

The first and last letters of some five-letter words are given below.
How many can you think of? To start you off, the first word could be HARSH.

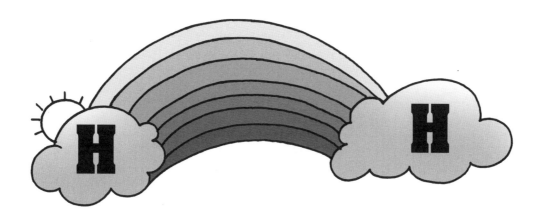

H <u>A</u> <u>R</u> <u>S</u> H

H _ _ _ H

**H _ _ _ H**

H _ _ _ H

H _ _ _ H

☺ Good:       1 – 2
☺ V. Good:        3
☺ Excellent:    4 – 5

17

# Animal Kingdom

It's a jungle in here! Study the list of animals, then look up, down, across and diagonally in both directions in the word grid and circle all that you find.

| E | R | O | S | L | S | D | U | S | B | Q | R | B | G | Z |
|---|---|---|---|---|---|---|---|---|---|---|---|---|---|---|
| H | J | Z | I | W | O | L | X | Z | K | L | Y | P | O | M |
| W | B | O | O | M | R | H | Y | V | W | L | S | E | T | H |
| B | N | O | R | A | E | B | X | P | D | S | M | N | B | H |
| R | L | A | E | X | C | I | P | B | W | D | A | P | X | V |
| V | Z | G | P | O | O | F | D | I | X | H | W | Z | X | G |
| O | O | Y | L | P | N | H | W | K | P | Q | O | K | B | S |
| D | R | K | N | C | I | G | A | E | I | F | C | T | I | C |
| V | B | E | D | Z | H | N | L | E | O | P | E | V | V | K |
| H | H | I | E | H | R | E | H | Y | U | T | Z | K | N | O |
| O | B | E | N | D | Z | V | T | H | J | W | I | M | Q | Z |
| R | K | U | A | V | Y | H | Q | C | D | Z | D | G | G | Z |
| S | X | D | C | E | C | N | M | U | K | J | R | C | E | B |
| E | Y | P | T | C | W | M | O | N | K | E | Y | V | F | R |
| H | S | G | J | D | U | N | H | G | B | G | Q | W | N | B |

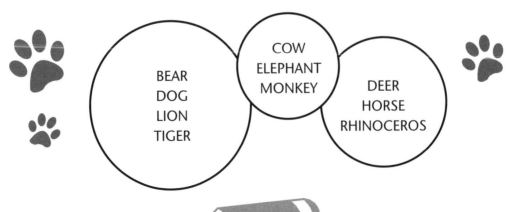

BEAR
DOG
LION
TIGER

COW
ELEPHANT
MONKEY

DEER
HORSE
RHINOCEROS

# Memory Test

Study this picture carefully for one minute,
then turn the page to answer some questions.

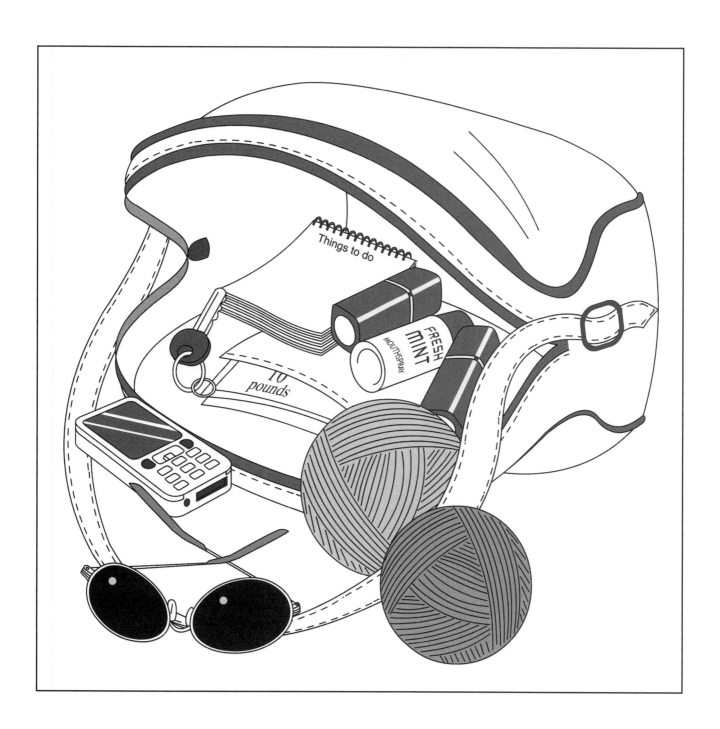

# Questions

How many things can you remember about the picture on the previous page? No peeking!

**1.** Are there any keys?

**2.** How many lipsticks are there?

**3.** Does the handbag have a long strap or a short handle?

**4.** Is there a yo-yo in there?

**5.** What is written on the note paper?

**6.** What is the denomination of the currency note?

**7.** What is the shape of the sunglasses – oval or rectangle?

**8.** Is the mobile phone ringing?

**9.** What flavour is the mouth spray?

**10.** Are there any needles in the knitting wool?

# Wonder Words

Starting from the top, move down each step adding one letter from the bottom row as you go, then rearrange all the letters around the 'O' to make a new word each time.

# Guessing Grid

Here's a mystery picture for you to identify.
Just draw what you see in each of the numbered boxes below into the
blank boxes that have the same number on the opposite page.

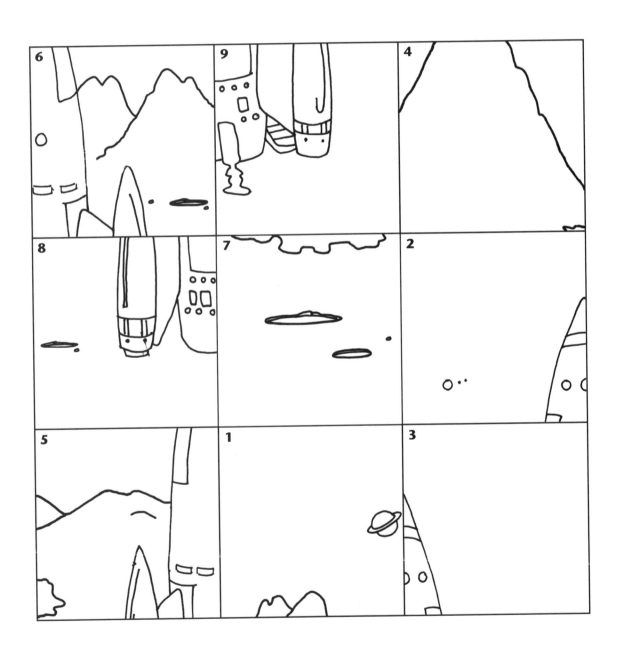

| | | |
|---|---|---|
| 1 | 2 | 3 |
| 4 | 5 | 6 |
| 7 | 8 | 9 |

# Lost Letters

These letters spell a word when they are put in the right order.
Track each letter along its path, then write it in its
correct place to find out what the word is.

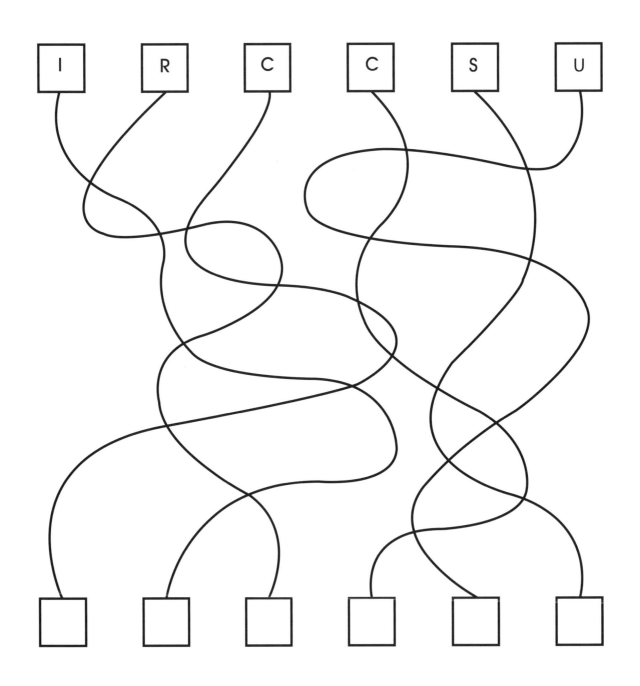

# Gender Bender!

Whose picture can you see in this image?
Is it a beautiful young lady or a man with a moustache?

25

# Tidy Town

This is a really tidy street, isn't it? However, some things have been
left lying about. Look at the list below and find them all.

Barcode

Bench

Coins

Dentures

Frankenstein

Hand mirror

Kennel

Plaster

Robot

Tortoise

# Take Your Pix!

How good are you at reading pictures? You had better be good!
Use the visual clues to fill in the words correctly in this picture crossword.

**Across**

③ 🍶

⑥ ☀️

⑤ 🪜

**Down**

① 🧅

④ 🏮

② 🐀

# Tale of Two Trainers!

There is a pair of identical trainers in this group.
Look carefully and draw a circle around the two that are exactly the same.

# Filling Station

The first and last letters of some five-letter words are given below.
How many can you think of? To start you off, the first word could be GRAPE.

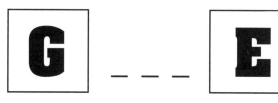

G _ _ _ E
G _ _ _ E
G _ _ _ E
G _ _ _ E
G _ _ _ E
G _ _ _ E
G _ _ _ E
G _ _ _ E
G _ _ _ E
G _ _ _ E
G _ _ _ E
G _ _ _ E

☺ Good:        1 – 4
☺ V. Good:     5 – 8
☺ Excellent:   9 – 12

# Double-D Muddle

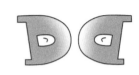

What do the words in the lists below have in common? They all have two 'd's in them! Look up, down, across and diagonally in both directions in the word grid and circle all that you find.

| R | B | R | W | E | L | L | S | Z | F | Y | I | Z | P | F |
| L | E | D | E | T | D | V | R | O | I | B | J | L | C | S |
| Q | J | L | P | D | Q | U | D | L | F | T | Y | V | P | C |
| R | M | R | D | H | D | D | B | S | T | S | P | A | G | D |
| V | B | I | F | D | E | E | G | W | G | W | P | X | W | E |
| T | P | D | U | R | O | E | N | S | E | M | D | Z | S | Z |
| L | U | D | I | K | L | T | R | Y | V | G | A | E | X | K |
| Q | S | L | F | D | E | L | D | D | A | T | T | Y | X | Y |
| P | H | E | D | Q | V | I | J | Q | G | T | G | S | W | N |
| H | C | U | U | Y | S | V | N | Z | E | C | M | J | I | O |
| U | F | W | A | D | D | L | E | V | L | B | J | W | M | A |
| Z | K | V | F | C | L | T | N | B | D | A | X | O | M | I |
| O | E | E | A | O | K | G | U | O | D | T | N | F | P | P |
| E | L | D | D | A | R | T | S | E | I | X | X | X | Q | P |
| W | F | R | A | F | S | W | N | Q | M | W | F | F | O | B |

FODDER
REDDEN
WADDLE

ADDLE
MIDDLE
TODDLER

FUDDLE
STRADDLE
RIDDLE

# Memory Test

Study this picture carefully for one minute,
then turn the page to answer some questions.

# Questions

How many things can you remember about the
picture on the previous page? No peeking!

**1.** What subject is being taught in class?

**2.** How many apples are on the table?

**3.** What date is written on the blackboard?

**4.** Is the teacher wearing spectacles?

**5.** How many girls have ponytails?

**6.** Are the boys' ties spotted or striped?

**7.** Are there any birds singing outside?

**8.** How many children know the answer?

**9.** Is someone watching from the hallway?

**10.** Is there a calendar on the wall?

# Word Triangle

Starting from the top, move down each step adding one letter
from the bottom row as you go, then rearrange all the letters
around the 'F' to make a new word every time.

| D | E | F | R | O | S | T |

# Guess Who?

Here's a mystery picture for you to identify.
Just draw what you see in each of the numbered boxes below into the blank boxes that have the same number on the opposite page.

| 1 | 2 | 3 |
|---|---|---|
| 4 | 5 | 6 |
| 7 | 8 | 9 |

# Letter Scramble

These letters spell a word when they are put in the right order.
Track each letter along its path, then write it in its
correct place to find out what the word is.

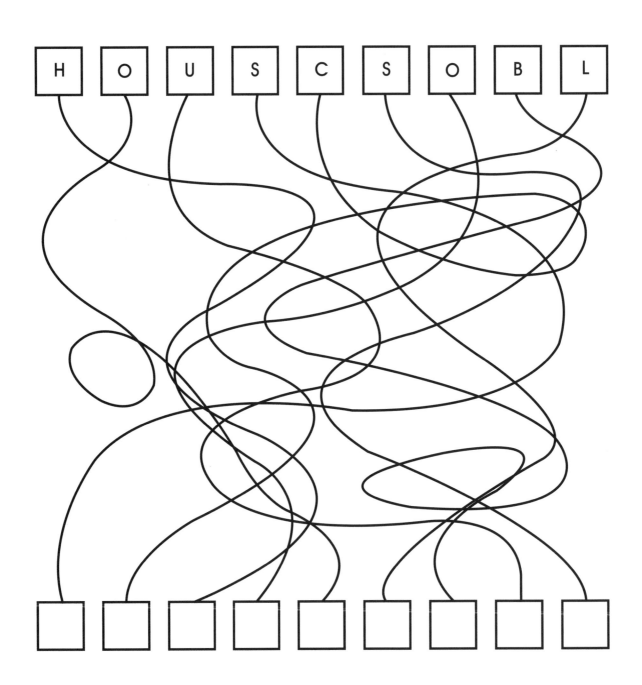

H   O   U   S   C   S   O   B   L

# Five-Legged Wonder!

Is this elephant so heavy that it has five legs instead of four?
Or are your eyes playing tricks? Check it out!

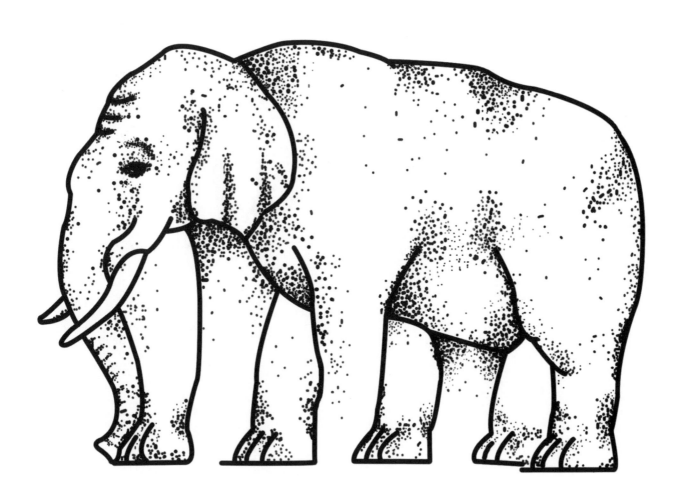

# Fun at the Park

The park is a great place to spend time. And while you are there,
can you find all the objects listed below that are hidden in this picture?

Balloon

Butterfly

Candyfloss

Dinosaur

Globe

Peacock feather

Piano keys

Shark fin

The digit 11

Umbrella

# See and Solve

How good are you at reading pictures? You had better be good!
Use the visual clues to fill in the words correctly in this picture crossword.

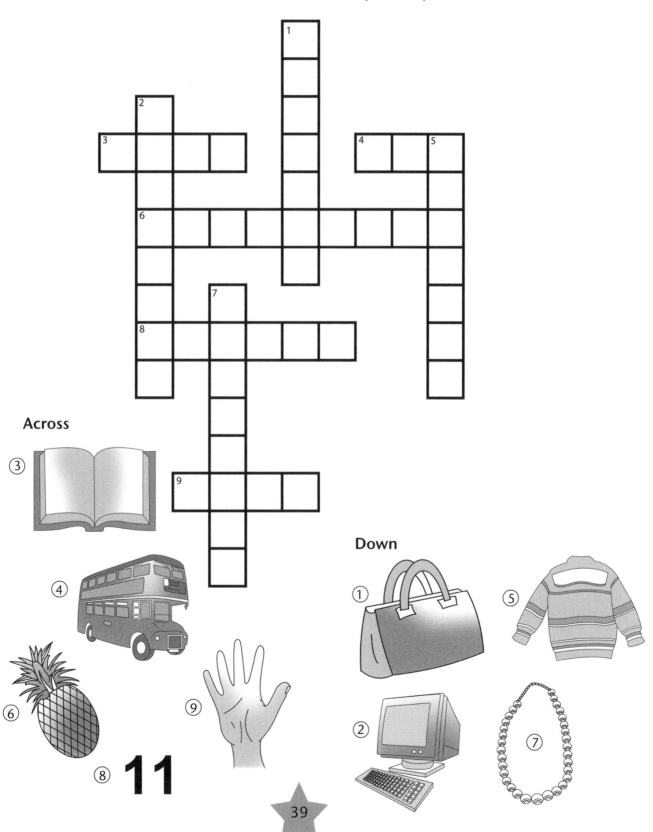

**Across**

③
④
⑥
⑧ **11**
⑨

**Down**

①
②
⑤
⑦

# Turkey Twins

There are two identical turkeys on this page.
Look carefully and draw a circle around the two that are exactly the same.

# First and Last

The first and last letters of some five-letter words are given below.
How many can you think of? To start you off, the first word could be OCCUR.

**O** _ _ _ **R**

O _ _ _ R

O _ _ _ R

**O** _ _ _ **R**

O _ _ _ R

O _ _ _ R

**O** _ _ _ **R**

O _ _ _ R

**O** _ _ _ **R**

O _ _ _ R

O _ _ _ R

☺ Good:      1 – 3

☺ V. Good:    4 – 7

☺ Excellent:  8 – 10

# Globetrotter

Get ready for a world trip! Take a look at the list of the countries given below. Look up, down, across and diagonally in both directions in the word grid and circle all that you find.

| M | N | F | E | B | F | Q | N | I | E | Y | K | T | J | W |
|---|---|---|---|---|---|---|---|---|---|---|---|---|---|---|
| T | O | O | Q | A | E | L | G | R | R | Z | N | C | T | Z |
| F | H | D | U | F | R | L | O | R | P | K | A | O | Y | D |
| R | H | J | G | G | P | P | G | A | C | N | I | M | M | N |
| J | C | I | B | N | A | O | F | I | I | S | L | C | A | R |
| I | Y | Z | E | G | I | R | N | Y | U | K | A | A | W | L |
| L | D | H | N | U | A | K | B | Z | D | M | R | N | G | Y |
| O | U | I | K | N | D | I | D | T | W | I | T | A | D | S |
| R | S | N | C | D | N | I | U | E | A | B | S | D | J | C |
| Y | S | E | C | X | S | A | C | L | T | U | U | A | Y | S |
| R | P | F | L | N | A | W | I | A | T | I | A | O | L | I |
| V | B | M | L | V | B | P | B | D | O | N | N | M | A | T |
| G | E | R | M | A | N | Y | K | I | N | I | V | U | T | Y |
| V | W | H | I | O | G | M | Y | M | P | I | R | H | I | C |
| Y | Z | C | G | U | V | V | U | J | Z | D | S | K | R | W |

AUSTRALIA     BELGIUM     CANADA

FRANCE     GERMANY     INDIA

ITALY     SINGAPORE     TAIWAN

UNITED KINGDOM

# Memory Test

Study this picture carefully for one minute,
then turn the page to answer some questions.

# Questions

How many things can you remember about the picture on the previous page? No peeking!

1. Is the pilot showing a 'Thumbs Up' sign?

2. Do the pilots have headphones on?

3. Is there a 'No Smoking' sign?

4. Can you see the landing strip?

5. What time is it?

6. Is the co-pilot wearing a full-sleeved shirt?

7. How many people are there in the picture?

8. Is there a glass of water in the picture?

9. Are both the pilots wearing caps?

10. What is written on the steward's sleeve?

Answers

## Page 3 – Dinosaur Duo

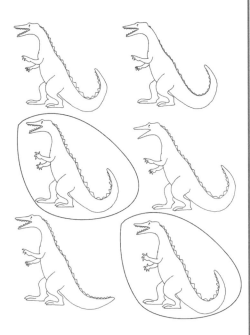

## Page 5 – Growing Wonder

## Page 6 – Fairytale Fuddle

## Page 8 – Memory Test

1. 3.55
2. Four
3. No
4. On
5. A toy duck
6. A scarf
7. Yes
8. Yes
9. Spring
10. Yes

## Page 9 – Seven Steps

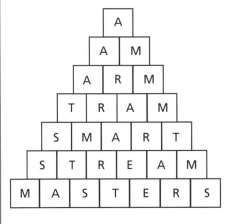

## Page 10–11 – Guess Who?

## Page 12 – Letter Leads
AEROPLANE

## Page 14 – Mum and Me

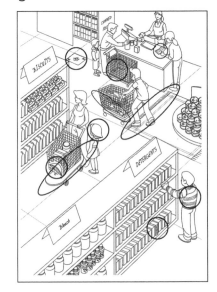

## Page 15 – Criss Cross

## Page 16 – Double Scoops

46

## Page 17 – Middle Muddle

1. HARSH
2. HITCH
3. HATCH
4. HUNCH
5. HEATH

## Page 18 – Animal Kingdom

## Page 20 – Memory Test

1. Yes
2. Two
3. Long strap
4. No
5. Things to do
6. 10 pounds
7. Oval
8. No
9. Fresh Mint
10. No

## Page 21 – Wonder Words

```
              O
           O     N
        C     O     N
     C     O     R     N
   A     C     O     R     N
 C     O     R     N     E     A
R   O   M   A   N   C   E
```

## Page 22–23 – Guessing Grid

## Page 24 – Lost Letters

CIRCUS

## Page 26 – Tidy Town

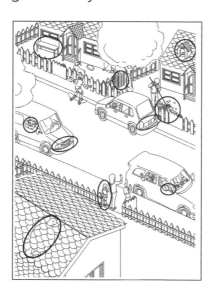

## Page 27 – Take Your Pix!

## Page 28 – Tale of Two Trainers!

## Page 29 – Filling Station

1. GRAPE
2. GOOSE
3. GRADE
4. GRATE
5. GLARE
6. GLAZE
7. GLIDE
8. GLOBE
9. GLOVE
10. GRACE
11. GRAZE
12. GUIDE

## Page 30 – Double-D Muddle

47

## Page 32 – Memory Test

1. History
2. Two
3. 25.9.06
4. No
5. One
6. Striped
7. Yes
8. Two
9. Yes
10. Yes

## Page 33 – Word Triangle

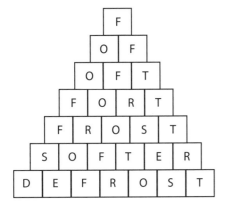

## Page 34–35 – Guess Who?

## Page 36 – Letter Scramble
SCHOOLBUS

## Page 38 – Fun at the Park

## Page 39 – See and Solve

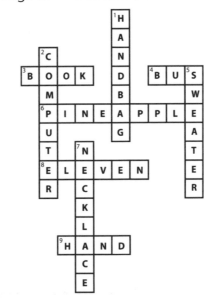

## Page 40 – Turkey Twins

## Page 41 – First and Last

1. OCCUR
2. ODOUR
3. OFFER
4. OLDER
5. ORDER
6. OTHER
7. OUTER
8. OWNER
9. OTTER
10. OILER

## Page 42 – Globetrotter

## Page 44 – Memory Test

1. No
2. Yes
3. Yes
4. Yes
5. 4 o'clock
6. No
7. Three
8. No
9. No
10. Air way